TURNING
the
PYRAMID
UPSIDE DOWN

A New Leadership Model

To Samantha and Jimm
Being with you both is
energizing.

yn

Marilyn D.
Jacobson, PhD.

For Mark

Diversion Books
A Division of Diversion Publishing Corp.
443 Park Avenue South, Suite 1008
New York, NY 10016
www.DiversionBooks.com

First Diversion Books edition January 2013

ISBN: 978-1-938120-94-7

Table of Contents

To lead people, walk beside them.

Lao Tzu, Father of Taoism

Introduction

As a professor of management for seventeen years and a consultant to scores of major businesses, I have witnessed a fundamental change in effective leadership practices.

For generations, the historic and prevailing certainty that organizations are pyramids, with the leadership at the top and workers at the bottom, no longer applies. What we have learned from today's most forward-looking companies is that only by turning the pyramid upside down can an organization in a global marketplace gain and secure competitive advantage. The lesson is that organizations must change significantly if they are to have a future in this rapidly changing world.

In the old paradigm, aspiring leaders were taught that the way to the top was to wring the most out of each of their employees. For a new reality in a new century, a different kind of leadership is required. Leaders must partner and collaborate with their employees to respond to escalating complexities and inspire new thinking and discovery of fresh ideas. The continuous pressure for innovation and new technologies means involving others at all levels within the organization. Employees cannot simply be instruments to achieve leaders' goals; they must be allowed and even encouraged to participate in the decision-making and be fully engaged in achievement of organizational goals.

Talent, skills, and leadership capability exist throughout the organizations and emerge when there is need and support. Since decision-making increasingly depends on multiple points of view and candid dialogue, the more perspectives the better. Therefore, restricting leadership to the top and rank and file to the bottom has lost currency; the reality is frontline employees collectively know more of what is crucial to wise policy making.

Globalization influences leadership in the U.S. in a number of ways in respect to buying or selling goods and mergers, acquisitions, and investments. Mastering more than one language and learning how cultures differ in significant ways so that meaningful relationships can be made happens only with effort, research, and sensitivity. The decision is to either train people internally or hire those from the outside who are skilled in these multiple areas.

Arab Spring and the worldwide clamor for voice in leadership affairs are mirrored in American workers' increasing dissatisfaction. Worldwide connectivity has brought attention to these uprisings, especially in terms of taking action to deal with what is perceived as despotic leadership. The response seen abroad is reflected in a widespread lack of trust within the U.S. workforce. Employees seek to have a voice. Managers are experiencing burnout and disillusionment. Morale is low. Because most corporations are hierarchical, many employees feel they are marginalized from what is most essential and, not incidentally, most interesting in the business. The irony is that while executives want thought leaders, they do not involve their employees, ask for their input, and most egregiously, do not share information. How can employees be expected to have a reliable thought or point of view? If they are not encouraged to think and are not invited into the dialogue, how can they contribute to discussion or decision-making?

The fundamental issue that leaders face in this global, high-tech environment is how to handle the complexities of strategic planning, decision-making, identifying and developing talent, building relationships and alliances, branding, pricing, marketing, and timing. Obviously, a single leader cannot undertake all this. Even the military that once served as the model for unilateral hierarchical leadership has changed. Partnering and collaboration are replacing command and control hierarchies. Cultures that promote thinking and empowerment provide incentives to contribute on a higher level. Breaking down the hierarchy and internal silos and creating an atmosphere that encourages engagement and attention to employee welfare are the prerequisites to meeting, welcoming, and thriving on change.

My experience consulting with leaders from a broad spectrum of industries informs the thesis of this book. Their stories reflect the need to partner and collaborate, develop new thinking, invite employees into the planning and decision-making process, encourage creative thought, and promote initiative.

They are a distinguished group. Because my consulting engagements extend for years and span a variety of fields (healthcare, retail, financial, manufacturing, service, legal, and government organizations), I have witnessed how leaders made decisions, what they learned, and what others may learn from them. Each story launches commentary based on the author's experience and research.

While these leaders' experiences and accomplishments take us to the frontier of a new era, their organizations are still basically top-down. The next bold step is to move away from command-and-control organization structures and toward flatter, inverted pyramid-type organizations. The future role of tomorrow's leaders will be quite different from the ones of yesterday. Instead of directing, leaders must develop, support, assist, and foster.

As a result, organizations will change significantly. Only if organizations redesign the structure and the culture to facilitate communication and productive interaction, at a level rarely seen outside of Silicon Valley, can the race to the future be won.

Leadership

The idea of turning the pyramid upside down may seem a bit radical because to be competitive in the new global economy, the magnitude of leadership change necessary defies any possibility that it be incremental. Escalating complexity due to such factors as technology and globalization, along with the continuing need to make the numbers while becoming ever more innovative, requires a kind of organization capable of extraordinarily high levels of purpose, commitment, and synchronicity.

It has been said that organizations are overmanaged and underled. Disappointment with leadership, as we have known it for many generations, has taken different forms. The current malaise in many organizations is a result of either too little leadership or the kind of leadership that has been modeled and passed along for generations, but is proving now to be grossly ineffective. That current breakdown is evident when executives lament the lack of thought leaders and workers lament their lack of autonomy and empowerment. This impasse has come about because leaders do not provide the kind of information and inclusion in decision-making that would produce thought leaders or in any way ensure an engaged workforce.

This is not a new phenomenon. When I was teaching MBA students, I would ask a class regarding the topic of motivation, "How would you like to be lead?" The most overwhelming responses were more autonomy, empowerment, support, access to viable resources, opportunities to collaborate on projects, and the ability to fully use their skills. When I turned the question around and asked (since many students had others reporting to them), "How do you lead?" The answers were provide direction, tell when things go wrong, correct mistakes, and follow up to ensure deadlines are met. It was sadly acknowledged that they were perpetuating the style of leadership they disliked. It is this style that needs an immediate overhaul.

When organizations are flatter and synchronicity is achieved, pyramids and hierarchies will be history. Synchronicity entered the business vocabulary in the late 1990s with Joseph Jaworski's book *Synchronicity: The Inner Path of Leadership*. The aptness is evident in the dictionary definition, "the coordination of events to operate a system in unison." Jaworski's interpretation is especially germane today. Imperative for him is the requirement that organizations be open to a new "world of possibilities." A second imperative is the need for people at all levels in organizations to participate in creating the future. For him, alignment is the critical path to success.

Progress to this alternative manner of leading has been slow but is picking up momentum. This will be apparent in the following pages as we trace the development of leadership ideas and practices. Environmental and organizational pressures have spurred some transitions without achieving more than slight deviations from what has become a norm.

It is this norm that needs to change. Ultimately it will be clear what is prompting profound change and what is needed not just to survive but also to thrive.

The Journey From the Great Man Theory to Post-Heroic Leadership

The passage described in this journey reveals the evolution in leadership beliefs and behaviors critical to understanding why dramatic steps need to be taken and the revolution that is inevitable.

Leaders Are Born

Dominating the leadership scene for many decades was the belief that a leader is born with certain traits or qualities which, because he or she is made of the "right stuff", will ensure that the organization will flourish. Accordingly, leaders were thought to be confident, self-assertive, visionary, and persistent in their search for new options. They relied on personal influence and the ability to shake up power bases, shape values, champion new ideas, and thrive on chaos. Many founders of organizations exemplified this brand of leadership. They bought and expanded businesses independently. Acting spontaneously with little pre-planning, they made things happen, which led to a spirit of excitement and buy-in from employees.

However, the need to shape order out of the chaos that came with this self-starting entrepreneurship initiated a chain reaction. While the leader remained at the top, a number of others were hired to produce systems, write policies and procedures, reduce risks, and find and maintain a status quo. The number of visionary leaders dwindled. The number of managers grew exponentially. As organizations expanded, divisions characterized by professional functions multiplied—

hence the advent of leaders of finance, production, distribution and personnel. Hierarchies were established. Command-and-control of separated areas became the norm, and silos developed with communication or cross- referencing between functional areas. Heroic, visionary leaders became rare and the pyramid broadened.

Managers are Different

Managers seek to be leaders, but how they function does not correspond to those qualities expected in leaders. As problem solvers whose primary task is to limit risk, pay attention to how things get done, and operate based on achievement of short-term results, they hardly seem like good candidates for visionary leadership. The proliferation of divisions based on functions and the emphasis on tactics and execution blur the leader/manager roles. The pursuit by managers of greater power and prestige through promotion and greater rewards changed the organization dynamic. Managers defined the span of control and accountability in order to quantify their domain. Motivation to move the organization as a whole began to shift to maintaining smaller, but expandable, units where order, control, and predictability could rule.

Transactional Leaders

As organizations begin to focus on short-term tactical results, rewards become contingent on the achievement of goals and objectives. The horizon for attaining strategic goals shortened considerably, from two to five years, to one year, and then to just one quarter of a year. So what do managers/leaders do? They adjust the goals, vision, and mission for practical purposes. If something is not broken, why worry about fixing it? Transactional leaders clarify goals and assign and designate the distribution of resources. "Management by Objectives" becomes a mantra. Big picture leaders, with dreams that can galvanize and unite an organization, morph into capable managers adept at meeting short-term objectives—generally based on the bottom line.

Situational Leadership

Increasingly, issues dividing managers and leaders have grown. A belief emerged that leaders could be made and leadership skills could actually be taught. Universities picked up on this and MBA and executive leadership programs proliferated. Behavior Theory differentiates between task-oriented leadership and relationship-centered leadership. Therefore, development of leaders depends on learning purpose-directed behaviors or people-directed behaviors. Contingency Theory brought attention to leaders adjusting to a situation.

Thus "Situational Leadership" was born. The leader's task is to diagnose the situation, the subordinate, and the style of leadership appropriate for each person. This formula has been useful mostly because it recognizes that leadership is not something you are born into, but it is what you are expected to do. Furthermore, it acknowledges that leaders should not be expected to have just one style of leadership, since obtaining results is more important than being authentic. Leaders are confronted by a formidable array of situations. Flexibility turns out to be the significant advantage.

Transformational Leaders

Those who seek to overcome the blurred lines between managers and leaders and who believe in the necessity of thinking and planning further out are attracted to what is called "transformational leadership." This new perspective re-emphasizes bigger picture, whole-organization performance results. Rewards are based on organization successes, not just attainment of division goals. As a result, there is renewed interest in the total workforce and how employees can be more effective. Attention is drawn to "followers." Motivation becomes the prevailing term for aligning the needs of employees with organization's strategic goals. Terms like trust, values, intellectual stimulation, and development (personal as well as skill-building) become part of the business lexicon. Incorporating these concepts and expediting the practices that evolved made organizational culture not just something that occurred on its own, but something that could and should be created.

A series of publications by CEOs and business theorists addressed the issue of followers and the importance of the reciprocal role of leaders and followers; leaders develop and empower while followers accept more responsibility, control, and accountability and gain a greater sense of ownership. In this progression, it is useful to note the influence of the "new science" of Chaos Theory, emanating out of the belief that there is harmony in the universe and organizations are part of the "complex network of people." This suggests that a leader's role is to promote the creation of an organization capable of learning and self-renewal.

Robert H. Miles, in an article written for the *Harvard Business Review (HBR)* in 2010, confronts the issues that spiral out of transformational efforts. The title "Accelerating Corporate Transformations (Don't Lose Your Nerve!)" almost tells the story; transformation efforts rarely work because they must be "bold and rapid to succeed." Therein lies the predicament. Most change efforts sponsored at the top fail; because the organization has become preoccupied with incremental improvement, there is uncertainty that the effort will stay the course, or the organization is already running at full capacity.

If mandated from the top, employees are vulnerable and hold back. If it fails, someone is likely to be blamed and will have to defend the indefensible. To use Miles' phrase, "you have to provide safe passage." This is difficult when managers and leaders both fear they will lose their job or their status in the change process. Miles concludes that the best method is "to deploy a rapid, high-engagement, all-employees cascade." Transformation launches must be bold and rapid to succeed, yet embedded in most organizations are various "speed brakes" that can slow progress to a crawl.

The primary reason transformations fail is that those that are successful still fall prey to a financial downturn or other perceived outside pressure. The organization then retreats to its comfort zone—business as usual before the change.

Teams

The modern formation of teamwork came about as a result of the quality movement started by W. Edwards Deming, a U.S. statistician and quality-control expert, who introduced it in Japan and eventually brought it to the U.S. Deming was largely responsible for Japan's Industrial Revolution. Initially the movement was a means to get employees to work together to identify and develop methods for increasing quality and productivity. In time, it became a way to get different levels of personnel to interact and consider broader strategic issues, make recommendations, and on occasion, implement their joint efforts.

Eventually project teams were formed, which were given resources and authority to make and execute decisions. His work led to Total Quality Management (TQM) and Six Sigma, which set even higher standards of quality and created a select group of employees known as Black Belts, trained in analytics and problem solving. Under this approach, cross-functional teams are viewed as critical to organizations and serve to break down the barriers that isolate functional workers from each other. The benefits of sharing information and expertise and accommodating new technologies are obvious, particularly as decision-making becomes more complex and requires inclusion of multiple skills and perspectives.

Teams have proven to be so productive that some people speculated that self-managed teams would make bosses obsolete. While that did not happen, some organizations did restructure to capitalize on the collective wisdom of team members drawn from different functions. Matrix organizations were created to maximize employee skills. Immediate results were positive; organizations benefited and the engaged team members gained insights from the information that was shared with them regarding business strategy and the empowerment that came with planning and executing. Over time, however, power issues intervened. While matrix structures still exist in certain industries, and the concept has followers, it did not generally take hold.

At the same time that cross-functional teams were developing relationships internally, those at the top of the organization were identifying global opportunities and securing alliances across the world. Suddenly, the business lexicon expanded to include "globalization," "sensitivity to foreign cultures," and being "savvy regarding new technologies and partnering." Whole new skill sets were needed, which some leaders quickly embraced and a few of the rank and file already possessed.

Post-Heroic Leaders

The movement away from heroic leaders has been continuous. Organizations know that they cannot wait until the right person with the right traits shows up. Increasingly there is doubt that even charisma and individual competences are enough to make a competitive difference. The inevitable question arises: Is it even possible for one person to possess the breadth of characteristics and competencies required to lead successfully? Some theorists explore the possibility that leaders need new traits or points of view. Two closely related proposals—one called Stewardship, the other Servant Leadership—elevate service over self-interest. Both recommend a redistribution of power, purpose, and reward. The titles are expressive of the intent; leaders need to reposition themselves and become supportive of others who have different sets of skills, knowledge, and experience. The shift suggests this is not about decreasing power for one person but increasing power for many people who collectively can achieve far more.

It is time to note that many people in the same organization share the heroic leadership attributes of energy, drive, conviction, intelligence, and commitment. So the questions must be restated: "To what extent and for what purposes do we need leaders? Do we need a different set of attributes? How do we find and hire those who can deal with the ambiguity presented in arenas outside their experience? How can they master subtle and nuanced decision-making to arrive at a definitive conclusion? Or should we deploy people, those already within the organization, in a different way?"

A concept called "Self Leadership" suggests that more than one of those highly qualified, talented people within the organization is ready to emerge as a leader when their expertise is required. Some organizations have discovered that these individuals exist when their unique capabilities enable them to step up and provide leadership in a crisis. Must a crisis occur before talent is identified and utilized?

According to Pamela Butler, PhD, author, and clinical psychologist, if we ever hope to be effective leaders of others, we must first be effective leaders of ourselves. To better understand the process of self-leadership and how we can improve our capability in this area, we should first explore the meaning of the word "leadership."

There are a seemingly endless number of definitions and descriptions of leadership—largely as a result of the vast number of people who have researched and written on the subject (and their equally vast and differing viewpoints). All of these descriptions have some merit. However, in focusing on the idea of self-leadership, perhaps the most useful definition of leadership is simply "a process of influence."

Self-leaders require feeding, not from 24-hour kitchens provided by some organizations to keep people sequestered, but from data and intelligence regarding the industry, the environment, and what competitors are doing. They seek access to material and people who will share information and industry know-how. They are beginning to look like thought leaders, always learning and open to opportunities to contribute at a higher level.

The existing chasm between leaders who make decisions and the others who execute them suggests that having a world of possibilities requires some fundamental shifts in the minds and methods of those referred to as leaders and their subordinates. Boundaries need to be torn down so that the commitment is to the whole organization—not just to its parts. Synchronicity, with its emphasis on dialogue and commitment, is a more direct and meaningful way of demonstrating the value of collectivity and the consequences of not acting swiftly in the midst of an environment of severe turbulence, but also enormous opportunity.

Military

You might think, as I did when writing this book, that the military is a most unlikely venue to look to for a new approach to leadership. Reading an air force internal document with a commentary by Lieutenant Colonel James Jacobson, entitled "The Inverted Pyramid of Leadership," corrected that hypothesis. The author saw his sector experiencing the same issues as those in business, and he proposed ways to respond to change, similarly to those advocated in this book.

The thesis of his article is that when there is an inverted pyramid, the leader asks, "What can I do to help you?" Or "What do you need to be successful?" and then provides the resources and freedom to make the best decision.

After many generations of command and control, all branches of the armed forces are to various degrees, "powering down" (as it is referred to in a *Harvard Business Review* web exclusive). Business related publications, plus memoirs and interviews with current and retired military officers, reveal unprecedented changes in how leaders expect troops to behave. Extreme conditions as encountered in Iraq and Afghanistan show that modern warfare requires new skills.

Since those on the front line have more information regarding what is happening, they need to be either decision makers or decision influencers. Training, therefore, builds skills in how to *think* about what to do when encountering the enemy (or possible enemy). Making decisions without checking with command marks a major difference from the past. The other different, most noteworthy difference is that command is now open to challenge, and indeed expects, trainees to speak up, ask questions, and offer alternatives. The changes in the military are having an impact on management leadership. The benefit of flatter, more inclusive organizations is being demonstrated under the most difficult of circumstances. Organizations pummeled by change can look to the military as a model. Some of the most challenging issues, such as dealing with ambiguity, highlight the similarities. For instance, ambiguity is generally dealt with at the top.

Increasingly those without high rank in both industry and the military must not make hasty decisions. They must take time to consider many options and select an optimal one. Responsibility for creativity, usually thought to be a higher-level responsibility, is now recognized as everyone's to consider. The belief that anyone in an organization is able to assume leadership when the situation requires it, is outside hierarchical thinking but is gaining credibility.

Colin Powell, former Secretary of State and retired four-star general in the U.S. Army, emphasizes in a biography by Oren Harari (*The Leadership Secrets of Colin Powell*) the need for involving and engaging every mind. Leaders, he insists, must "check their egos." Trust is needed across the ranks. He urges "passionate curiosity" and suggests, "native ingenuity needs to be tapped." There needs to be an "appetite for change."

Military and business organizations are struggling with the same issues, namely: inclusion, trust, and change. The dilemma centers on solving problems on the spot. There is rarely an opportunity for deliberation or consultation; no policy and no single person can be relied upon when crises occur.

There is much to be learned from each other. As those who have served in the new military become an expanding talent pool for organizations, this interface could prove mutually beneficial.

Chapter One: Using Power to Empower

During a one-on-one meeting with Ann Yee-Kono, Executive Vice President of Investment Operations and Technology with Ares Management, we spoke about her prominence in the firm and her participation in Fortune's *Most Powerful Women Summit*.

She asked me what attributes I thought were needed to be a truly outstanding CEO. I replied with a few points, but I have continued to think about her question ever since. She is a rare example of how leadership adds value in a dramatically growing and changing organization. Her emphasis on both individual and team development is what smart leaders must adopt.

Ann started her career at Ares by implementing a global technology platform. While the system proved to be highly effective, it was the thorough, dedicated manner in which she conducted the project that won her praise. As a positive agent for change, she has built a multi-skilled team that is entrepreneurial, disciplined, and accurate. She cross-trains people so that they are continuously learning and being challenged. Her reports describe her as someone who motivates them and differentiates the way she works with individual team members.

She is very conscious of being a leader with all the responsibility that it entails, especially in a company like Ares, which consists of many separate and distinct businesses. As a private equity firm, Ares has several partners, each with unique staffing and team requirements. Being knowledgeable and staying on top of all aspects of the firm is critical. Ensuring that each of her team members is capable and reliable in their effort to support their partners' increasing demands is also a constant challenge.

The dynamic growth of the firm has necessitated a continuing search for new employees. Training them to get up to speed quickly is essential. They must be qualified to answer partner questions with confidence and accuracy. She delegates, empowers, encourages, and models collaboration.

She stays ahead of the curve by accessing new technology, reducing processing time, and predicting talent that will be needed. One of her techniques for accomplishing this is a service survey completed by partners regularly to learn ways to improve.

Ann is attentive to organizational nuances and quick to see implications. Knowing the industry and reading the environment is enhanced by her networks outside the firm. As part of a consortium of asset managers, attendance at conferences, plus watching what competitors are doing helps her maximize what she can achieve in her position.

While her question regarding the attributes of a CEO suggests she is thinking ahead, it is also evident that what is sought is neither power nor influence, but more interesting and challenging work in the arena where decisions with the biggest risks and rewards are made.

Empowering Others and Networking

Giving up power by empowering others is a hurdle for some who equate leadership with "being on top." Advancement to the C-Suite connotes both title and role. While turning the pyramid upside down is a major paradigm change, one current leader said, "I never had so much power until I started giving it away."

Each firm has its own culture, but some individuals

deliberately work at shaping their own path to leadership in their division. Building high-functioning teams is one way that leaders free themselves to think, act, and contribute strategically. Flexible, agile, and cross-trained team members are also learning that they can play a critical role, not only in developing themselves but their peers as well. This reduces competition and encourages a united approach to advancing the business and themselves. While most teams are designed to be implementers, not decision-makers, increasingly the promise for teams is to take their knowledge and experience to the next level, which is analysis, project design, and delivery.

What Ann (and others profiled for this book) also emphasize, is the keen importance of networking. They claim this connects them to people with expertise and mindsets outside their organization and their industry. They are exposed to alternative ways of visualizing the future and addressing common problems. Creative solutions surface. Through association memberships and participation in formal or informal discussion groups, individuals begin to think outside of cultural mores and open up to new ways of framing issues that can lead to less biased and more informed decision-making.

Chapter Two: Ask, Don't Tell

Norman Axelrod started his career at Bloomingdale's. Like many in the retail industry, he had mentors, worked hard, and traveled extensively. After thirteen years, he was one of eight individuals named by Marvin Traub, the legendary CEO of Bloomingdale's, as a prospective successor. Instead, Norman was approached to be the CEO and Chairman of Linens 'n Things and accepted that challenge.

He took on the job with considerable experience as a merchant but with little knowledge of real estate, human resource management, or finance. Never afraid to ask for assistance from experts, he developed a network outside of Linens of "smart people" from whom he could learn. He maintained and utilized his network for years. From those world-class people he learned "little problems go away."

Three months after becoming CEO at Linens, Norman spoke with a former mentor who asked him about his priorities in his new position; Norman presented a twelve-point list with people being number eight. His mentor suggested that number eight should be number one, and this became a defining moment for Norman and the basis of his leadership style.

He grew the business from 143 stores and revenues of $183 million to 590 stores (24 in Canada) with revenues of $2.9 billion. From the beginning, he earned respect for his abilities as a merchant. He was viewed as a charismatic leader who had much to teach others. He could be tough and provocative, but employees claimed they were always learning from him.

Initially when he saw a problem he told others how to solve it. A major epiphany occurred when he realized he needed to tell less and ask more if he was to maximize the talent and skills of those who worked for him. This was such a revelation that "ask, don't tell" became his mantra.

At a recent meeting, we were talking about what he learned from his tenure at Linens. He started with his mantra and to emphasize his point, called his son A.J., who is a consultant with Accenture. Norman asked him to relate what the most important principle for an executive to know is and handed his cell phone over. Without further prompting, A.J. repeated the mantra.

Norman was informed that when store managers were confronted with a difficult decision they would ask themselves, "What would Norman do?" The speaker expected him to be pleased. Norman quickly replied this was not good news; he had come a long way in understanding the power of asking, not telling.

When he took Linens 'n Things public, he had to spend most of his time outside of the office and the stores, leaving his employees to run their businesses without his oversight. They stepped up to the challenge and excelled.

Norman created an Office of the President, composed of four executives. This was a departure from the business norm, but he saw the benefits and realized that if it was to succeed, he must give over authority and decision-making and let them make critical decisions without his intervention. According to Norman, smart people get even smarter when they are empowered.

The breakthrough in asking and listening in business settings is now reflected in what is called "adaptive leadership" in the military: setting a direction, but not micromanaging, in order to give people freedom to improvise. The discovery that those closest to the front lines have the most knowledge has broken down the stereotype that the military is "tell, don't ask." General Powell has said that "listening, questioning, problem-solving and collective ingenuity are now required in the military."

Chapter Three: Magic for Macy's

Macy's advertising slogan, since the stores from different divisions all took the Macy's name, has been "The Magic *of* Macy's." What the Logistics and Operation Division has accomplished *for* Macy's has been "magic"—not like Houdini's, but the result of hard work, people development, cutting-edge technology, setting exceptionally high goals, and achieving them.

Peter Longo, President of Macy's Logistics and Operations, started his career at Bloomingdale's. After eleven years, he was promoted to President of a fledgling organization within Federated Department Stores (of which Bloomingdale's was a part) to handle the huge task of getting merchandise to all the divisions in a timely and cost-effective manner.

Over the years the task grew exponentially, especially after the merger with May Company, which doubled the size of Macy's. This came at a time when technology advancement, connected with direct-to-consumer ordering and delivery, demanded exceptional leadership. Macy's Logistics and Operations has met and exceeded everyone's expectations each year.

Supply chain and logistics, according to Peter, is all about "moving stuff" from manufacturers to stores and distribution to customers. There are enormous complexities as the process involves reaching goals and benchmarks, while linking dollars and service levels. It requires a constant juggling of people, processes, and technology. When optimized, these three elements create what Peter calls the "turbocharger" due to the truly superlative results achieved. The technology has to be cutting-edge and world class. To expedite the process, Logistics introduced the Six Sigma process, which relies on teams to determine the absolute best means to achieve goals using a problem-solving approach.

Peter has a way of setting organization goals that seem impossible, yet each year the team meets and usually exceeds the desired outcomes. This effort has continuously raised the bar for Logistics and Operations, not only within Macy's but in the entire industry as well.

Peter describes his selection process as topgrading and hiring the best, providing a learning/growing environment, and ensuring that there is diversity of experiences and backgrounds. The fundamental belief in hiring the best people and setting lofty benchmarks through the years has produced a relentless focus on being the best in the field. Being a learning organization pushes people to know that they must stretch to get better and promotes recognition that the organization will invest in them. The result is loyalty and high performance.

Peter believes that by showing confidence in people, you can ask them to do what you know they have the ability to accomplish. The result for Macy's Logistics and Operations is double-digit growth and the intention to be "best in the American field" and best of its kind in the world. The year 2011 was the sixteenth best year in a row. There has never been a year that did not improve upon the previous one.

Peter looks to Jim Collins and the "Big Hairy Audacious Goal" in his book, *Good to Great: Why Some Companies Make the Leap...and Others Don't* as a model. He maintains that an organization that does not have challenging goals stands still.

Peter has capitalized on technology and leadership within Logistics to great advantage, first for Federated, and now for Macy's and Bloomingdale's. This combination is clearly the foundation of a competitive organization.

Peter's focus on Six Sigma and planning has been complemented by the focus on people development. Kevin Hart, the HR officer from Logistics' inception, knew the business thoroughly, counseled, coached and mentored. He also served as the representative and liaison throughout Macy's. Kevin retired in 2011, and his handpicked successor, Daniel Ginsberg, is continuing the successful leader development approach, along with positioning executives to be effective coaches.

Being first with new technology is critical in the competitive retail world. First it was the bar code, and soon it will be Radio Frequency Identification (RFID). The technology had been described as a solution without a problem. Macy's Logistics and Operations is taking the lead internationally with retailers in designing ways to use the RFID technology. Now millions of dollars will be saved with inventory control.

Tom Cole, Chief Administrative Officer for Macy's and the architect of Logistics, maintains that great leaders create the future, and he credits the success of Macy's Logistics and Operations to passion, precision, and people.

Chapter Four: Streamline and Simplify

I met Fareed Khan in 2002, which was early in his career at USG Corporation (United States Gypsum). He was asked to lead a group consisting of ten of the "best and brightest" managers to determine what should be done to prepare and position the company for the year 2020. The team ultimately dispersed as the members were promoted elsewhere. Working with the team, I learned to value the wisdom of anticipating the future and positioning the organization favorably. This insight has been an important part of my consulting and coaching, and I expect it will be even more critical for future leaders.

During 2007, while still at USG, the home business was in a freefall.

The story is best told by Fareed:

"Building systems was about $3.6 billion in sales when I was named president. It declined by above a billion dollars in sales over an 18-month period, due to the changes in the market. EBITDA (Earnings before Tax and Amortization) fell by a billion dollars over the same period, due to falling demand and a pricing collapse in wallboard.

The problem the business was facing was an unprecedented drop in demand not seen since the depression. New housing, repair and remodel, and later the commercial construction market all collapsed, and we had no idea how low they would fall. The challenge was that we had an asset intensive manufacturing business with numerous plants and vertically integrated business models, so we had plants, mines, and ships all operating at less than 50 percent utilization. We also saw prices collapse in wallboard and our customers facing intense competitive pressure.

We needed to move fast in an unpredictable and rapidly changing market. We also had a diverse business mix and many products that were being impacted in different ways by the downturn.

The problem with our functional structure was that it was a "one size fits all" model, and the different businesses needed different strategies that would have to be shaped and executed in different ways. Decision-making was quick for large businesses like wallboard, but small businesses did not get enough focus and many were in decline.

The new matrix structure increased accountability, decentralized P&L leadership, and allowed emerging leaders to run sizable businesses with more autonomy than the company had ever done. Keeping manufacturing, marketing, and sales as shared functions allowed us to keep operating discipline and present one face to the market.

The organization was completed just before the downturn accelerated, and it really worked. Leaders emerged and stepped up in ways that were remarkable. Decision-making was fast. There was true accountability and ownership, and the various leadership teams developed deep bonds and created mini-cultures of their own. The connectivity of shared services and the tight and frequent leadership interactions kept us all aligned.

This allowed us to make gut-wrenching cuts in some areas, while investing in others. We managed to achieve record margins (profit per unit sold) in almost all businesses despite a top line in freefall.

The structure was loose and decentralized, but because of the matrix nature, we risked conflict and bureaucracy. To avoid this, we used simple three-page business operation plans and a scorecard. We forced "speed-dating" sessions, so businesses and support functions could spend time and understand and resolve competing priorities. The team structure allowed people to really focus on their business. We met with business and functional teams frequently to review results using one-page scorecards. No PowerPoint!

The scorecard, business plan, and meeting cadence streamlined decision-making and drove efficient ways for the businesses and support functions to get what they needed quickly. It was a simple approach, but very powerful."

As a leader, Fareed points to three "lessons." 1) What is needed is a crystal clear understanding of what the issue is in a simple statement. 2) Have a simple plan to address issues, which is understandable to all. 3) Make early predictions and then achieve them.

He has taken this approach with him into his role as CFO at United Stationers.

Engagement

Engagement is becoming the watchword in many organizations as they realize the benefits to a committed workforce. Restructuring an organization to unleash energy and increase involvement was successful at a 200-bed hospital in Santa Cruz, California.

After a series of personnel changes, a new CEO at Community Hospital of Santa Cruz decided she needed a consultant. When I showed up to meet with her and her direct reports, I was handed a list of twenty-two people. It was clear that the hospital was top-heavy, and restructuring had to be the first consideration. After many interviews and considerable discussion, two structural models were presented for consideration. The whole group met to decide on one. Instead they asked if there were others they should consider. The next week, five different models (with pros and cons) were presented, and diagrams were hung on the walls of a conference room. The group came to consensus on a cluster management design, unusual in hospitals at that time. It featured a flatter organization, allowing greater communication and ease in launching new products and services. The new structure was put into place with enthusiasm and a sense of ownership, even though many lost their leadership status as part of the hospital management.

Rarely is an organization tested in quite the fashion this one was. Within two years after the reorganization, Santa Cruz was devastated by an earthquake that caused massive damage. The hospital responded beyond any possible expectation. Since the only other hospital in the vicinity had been leveled, the full burden for care was placed on Community. Helicopters landed one after another, patients were brought in by ambulances, and the three teams formed as a result of the organization they designed, worked successfully together. The hospital drew praise from a grateful city.

Chapter Five: Numbers vs. Newness

Walking through the building where Beth Kaplan's office and those of her team were housed, I was immediately drawn by the sound of laughter and the unexpected sight of a pulsating light hanging outside an office. Clearly a meeting was taking place and the participants did not want to be disturbed. Giving in to my temptation to listen permitted insight into how a truly engaged team functions creatively. The camaraderie, mutual respect, and interest in different viewpoints, as well as the obvious energy demonstrate Beth's ability to get people involved.

Beth was at Procter & Gamble, Rite Aid, Bath & Body Works, and most recently, she was President of GNC. Throughout her career, she was "parachuted into circumstances where a fresh look at strategy was needed." She worked at integrating cultures with merged companies to drive innovation. She introduced a more modern feel or repositioned a company to be more contemporary and thereby more competitive in its industry. Modernizing is her forte as she reinvigorates and innovates by adding new products into the pipeline.

Beth brings a strong belief in the power and passion that a highly engaged team contributes to an organization. She creates a work dynamic that gets people committed to working hard to achieve mutual goals.

She insists that everyone wants to be part of the process; those left out are demoralized. People want to be valued and perceived as good enough to be part of the dialogue. She believes that each person is extraordinary in his or her own way and wants to be involved. Spirits are high when group members see themselves as part of a quality group.

Innovation, she believes, is hard and takes patience. Introducing a new strategy requires total alignment. It is a time when huge expectations emerge and the need to reconcile the budget and meet the targets takes over. Unfortunately when one innovation fails, all those that follow are constrained by fear of another failure.

One major risk in retailing is related to inventory, which can produce shifts from thinking too big or too small, which is common in other industries. Some organizations choose a new strategy that starts small but is prepared to move swiftly to meet demand if it occurs. According to Beth, the key point in doing innovation well is "developing a product or service strategy and a commercial strategy that appeals to the customer." This involves understanding where the customer is, where opportunistic white spaces are, and how to position the product accordingly. Responding quickly, she maintains, is closely related to the organization's supply chain: making and delivering component parts in a cost-effective manner.

Beth also values the culture of an organization which she feels can be important by providing an ethical framework for employees. They come to realize how culture shapes leadership, decision-making, and resource allocation. Culture is also context or environment, which she shapes by ensuring there are few cubicles and many conference spaces and round tables so that hierarchy is not apparent.

Creativity and Innovation

In his 2012 book, *The Idea Factory: Bell Labs and the Great Age of American Innovation*, Jon Gertner eloquently expresses one of the critical issues of our time regarding innovation: "Most feats of sustained innovation cannot occur in an iconic garage or the workshop of an ingenious inventor. They occur when people of diverse talents and mind-sets and expertise are brought together, preferably in close physical proximity where they can have frequent meetings and serendipitous encounters."

Silicon Valley has changed the perception of success, which links being competitive with creativity and innovation. The late Steve Jobs knew what constituted newness and how he could develop a process to achieve it over and over. According to his biographer, Walter Isaacson, great innovators "applied imagination to technology and business." There has been little imagination visible in corporate America. The really important question is: Can America invent its way back?

The key to Jobs' success is that he knew those people who he identified as A Players, and they were the only ones he wanted to work with. He reasoned correctly that A Players like to work with other A Players, and he was smart enough to bring them together at Apple to work with him and each other. The work itself was attractive, even riveting, and Jobs' passion and purpose were inspirational. Isaacson quotes Jobs: "Creativity comes from spontaneous meetings, from random discussions...soon you are cooking up all sorts of ideas." In the physical environments he designed for his employees, he created opportunities for interaction and synergies.

Chapter Six: Let's Get Engaged

Brian Lemon served as CEO of Vanguard MacNeal Hospital, the Chicago-area flagship of investor-owned Vanguard Health Systems from 2006 to 2012. It had previously been a standalone hospital in the late 1990s; at that time, a visionary board and senior management team saw that the hospital's future was "finite" and realized that being part of a larger system was inevitable. They decided to take the initiative while in a position of strength. Subsequently they became part of Vanguard, which seemed to be a perfect fit. As CEO, Brian reported to Vanguard but soon found the company's financial emphasis was not in sync with his views. He left to work as CEO at another hospital.

He returned to MacNeal as CEO in 2006. In the meantime Vanguard had been recapitalized, and a new President with a different philosophy more aligned with patient quality and safety was on board. Brian's strong belief in a highly engaged workforce was also shared with the new Vanguard leadership. He had found a "comfortable home."

The management plan for MacNeal is based on a sophisticated one-page scorecard, in which the goals are stated and assigned measurable targets. Management is highly sensitive to community needs, hospital development, and environmental stewardship, with particular emphasis on employee engagement. For the past four years, Brian has been using Gallup tools and the Employee Engagement Survey to highlight the drive for improvement. This approach is obviously effective; Vanguard has won the Gallup Great

Workplace Award two years in a row.

Brian links the focus on employee engagement with improved performance, but also as a way of staying competitive in a tough environment. He maintains it has made the hospital stronger.

His message to employees is to be "persistently mindful." It is part of a culture that urges and protects everyone in the hospital to point out misses before they become problems. The goal is to learn lessons when the stakes are low. As a result, negative safety events have been reduced significantly from one event in a week to two in five months.

As part of a Vanguard mission of "Health for Life," mapping exercises starting with senior executives cascaded down to each hospital. Brian's summary of the results in MacNeal started with a surprise; the food service staff picked up on it immediately. They made providing healthier food their challenge and used pricing as the wedge. Their first step was to draw interest to what is healthy by lowering the price of healthy food. They got rid of the fryers and installed stir-fry pots; the stir-fry stations flourished. In time, sweetened drinks were gone along with other unhealthy offenders. It was gratifying to see a service area make important changes that they designed and executed.

He points with pride to his senior leadership team. He says they are "the best team ever," a claim supported by their accomplishments—the highest score in the Vanguard system in quality and safety, Magnet Recognition® from the ANCC, a Gold Standard earned by less than 10 percent of national and international hospitals, and the hospital's steady progress towards its goal of virtually eliminating serious safety events. In his last two years at MacNeal, the hospital was recognized by Vanguard as having both the best Quality & Safety performance and the best financial performance.

In September 2012, Brian was recruited by Cadence

Health, the health system created through the merger of Central DuPage Hospital (CDH) and Delnor Hospital, to be President of CDH and Executive Vice President of Cadence Health. Cadence Health employs more than 6,100 professionals, providing care across an interdependent network of healthcare organizations. Central DuPage Hospital—a nationally recognized 313-bed facility located in the suburbs of Chicago—has been listed by Thomson Reuters as a top 100 hospital in the U.S. and has an extensive network of related healthcare facilities.

Both hospitals have achieved ANCC Magnet Recognition® for excellence in nursing services. Central DuPage Hospital has a legacy of excellent care and service to the community.

The challenge for Brian is to stay on the path of extraordinary excellence. Brian wants his imprint to be "ultra safety." Hospitals everywhere are plagued by safety issues, and while advances have been made, there is more to be done. The word "safety" addresses two situations: one is when something has gone wrong, and patient families have issues to which hospital executives and doctors listen and respond; the other aspect of safety is when mistakes occur. This also calls for listening, learning, and responding so that the number of safety issues diminishes. However, even under the very best conditions safety can be compromised. Brian wants to be on the forefront of reducing the numbers of errors to the lowest point achievable.

Chapter Seven: U.S. Law Goes Global

How does one of the largest law firms in the world manage nine offices in the U.S., eight in Europe, and one in Asia? What does it take to maintain a strong clearly articulated culture and consistent leadership in such a vast organization? The answer is not what, but who. With Jeff Stone as Co-Chair of McDermott Will and Emery, one of the largest law firms in the world, the organization is thriving.

After McDermott was awarded the coveted *U.S. News and Best Lawyer* survey Tier 1 status across thirty-one of its practice areas, Jeff highlighted the "innovation and passion our attorneys bring to their profession every day" as the responsible factor. He points with pride to teamwork, mutual respect, and commitment. His conversation is punctuated with key words such as values, diversity, and social responsibility. It is clear that his point of view drives much of the organization.

There are many distinctive qualities to this law firm that aspires to be the best legal organization in the world: financial strength, numerous specialty areas, and diversity, to name a few. Most distinguishing is how management of this large and successful organization is enabled by a unique structure without one managing partner. Instead there are two co-chairs. Since there are few, if any, law firms that operate with more than a single person—a managing partner—at the top, this departure was obviously part of a deliberate effort to rewrite the rulebook in providing legal services globally.

The structure, which Jeff describes as a matrix, allows the two co-chairs and the four who lead business units, plus those who head practice groups to collaborate, coordinate efforts, and respond quickly. He has reevaluated almost every process and policy including such basics as billable hours, hiring, succession planning, and compensation. He believes that those who are informed and engaged will coalesce to align with the firm's strategic objectives. As a result, the firm can be nimble and responsive internally to partners and externally to clients.

Strategic goals tailored for offices in each country are enhanced by the expertise available within a matrix organization. Since objectives differ, it is a monumental advantage to have available people with knowledge, ability to plan, and wisdom regarding when to revise or abandon a strategy. Jeff is a strong voice for strategic thinking. The leadership role at McDermott is rigorous because client involvement is still expected. Leaders have to be supercharged and willing to invest time in multiple areas including pro bono work.

Capitalizing on innovation with respect to firm practices is a primary step in discovering and sustaining clients' pathways to newness in their respective industries. An example of this responsiveness is the Boot Camp for Private Equity. McDermott seeks to help equity firms anticipate the legal aspects of acquisitions or other deals they may consider.

If there is doubt regarding the business efficacy of Jeff's people-oriented approach, another persistent theme in his conversation is accountability. Expectations regarding performance continue to be high. What takes the sting out of challenging goals is the transparency McDermott has introduced. The Portal, as it is named, provides daily information regarding individual, office, and practice area performance across the firm. Transparency is also apparent in the many webinars keeping all the offices in touch with firm values, performance, plans, and goals.

Jeff's leadership demonstrates a dynamic process sensitive to change on multiple levels. The inclusive style that he practices keeps partners aligned with strategy and informed regarding available resources. He is altering a deeply entrenched legal paradigm from a time when partners did not want to be managed at all to appreciation of collective effort.

Embracing Change

Jeff's story is remarkably upbeat in the midst of tension and change in law firms in the U.S. and abroad. Some firms have merged domestically, others internationally; a few such as Dewey Ballantine, which started as a New York-based firm, merged with LeBoeuf, Lamb, Greene & MacRae. Ultimately Dewey & LeBoeuf, then a global law firm created in 1907, closed in 2012. Dewey's demise provides insights into how the practice of law is changing, primarily in terms of leadership, organization, structure, and culture. While McDermott is a noteworthy study in collaboration and involvement, Dewey depended solely on one person to be the decision-maker. That was its downfall.

The general manager of Dewey was able to inject toxic financial manipulations into the firm due to the age-old practice of lawyers willing to leave management to others, so that they might pursue their work without interruption.

Gradually, attorneys and law firms are realizing that a vastly competitive market is changing every aspect of law, including law as a business. In that paradigm, attorneys are viewed as a commodity to be outsourced. Associates are needed but not developed. Partners look for guarantees. There is a serious lack of communication. Management in firms has been accused of causing a corrosive culture where partners are either rainmakers or (to their peril) not.

Within the last few years, law firms have realized that as trusted advisors to businesses, they need to think like business leaders. In order to better serve their clients they must understand their issues. To do this, they need to reorganize themselves to build trust internally and externally. At McDermott, introducing the team concept increased responsiveness to business issues. They are able to serve their clients with increased sensitivity especially with respect to risk, strategic planning, and human resources.

Attributes of those providing leadership within growing legal firms start with a structure that permits and actually promotes input from partners, associates, and staff. A law firm profits dramatically when there is consensus in decision-making and informed and continuous communication.

Chaper Eight: From Waste to Wellness

I have followed Jenny Gumm's passage from a young woman with great promise to an exceptional team leader who discovered the productivity possible with a confident and committed group. Advancing in hierarchical companies, she showed concern for people and created opportunities for their development.

Jenny joined Waste Management in 1988 as a financial analyst. She then was selected to be the Assistant Controller for an operating location. When she was appointed team leader of a group that was charged to bring all the accounting locations into a single center, she learned how meaningful teams can be and how to lead a team entrusted with a monumental task. This led to the complete reengineering of the IT Systems. Her title changed to VP of Information Systems and Reengineering for Waste Management. After Waste Management merged with USA Waste, she outsourced all of IT and enabled most people to stay with the outsourced organization.

Jenny's next position was CIO at GE Capital Rail Services. Her timing was fortuitous, immediately following Y2K. There was tremendous pent-up demand for IT. She restructured the department and created the position of Relationship Manager to ensure that each part of the business received the assistance needed. As her focus shifted to E-commerce, she found ways to provide exemplary customer service. The existing GE Capital leadership program, which rotated senior managers, was a plus for managers but left those in divisions without the same opportunity to be promoted. She recognized and rewarded those in IT and helped them attain visibility that was previously lacking.

She was asked to serve on a team for GE Capital that led to her award as an "Outstanding Person." In her first year she had been nominated as one of GE Capital's top 1-2 percent.

A hiatus after leaving GE Capital allowed her time to reprioritize. She had experienced the command and control style at Waste Management and from project experiences learned what people can accomplish when they are engaged.

Her strong emphasis on the people side of business led her to start an Ed.D. program at Pepperdine University. Not surprisingly, work on her Ed.D. dissertation is about wellness and corporate America's need to appreciate the value of health and work-life balance.

Her research and personal experience has enabled her to see the connection between stress and both physical and mental health. She maintains that the corporate world denies the fact that work is draining, and that in dealing with their workforce organizations, they must see and care for the whole person. The cost of mental and physical breakdown is high. Attention to wellness, she says, can lead to more creative, innovative, and less stressed employees. She is currently starting a wellness business and has completed a pilot program.

The January/February 2012 issue of *Harvard Business Review* is dedicated to wellness. A number of points of view are explored, including degrees of happiness. Jenny has made wellness a personal priority as she establishes the link between being healthy in mind and body and increased effectiveness on the job.

Happiness

"The Happiness Factor" article, part of an issue dedicated to *The Value of Happiness: How Employee Well-Being Drives*

Profits starts with the obvious question: "Why write about happiness when so much of the global economy is still in a funk and people are manifestly unhappy across the world?" We have become accustomed to metrics based on revenues and profitability. If we step away from GDP as the baseline for measuring success and start to think forward to a more holistic approach to profitability, then health, education, and political freedom become critical parts of the equation.

If we could take another step forward, we would include the work of behavioral economists, psychologists, and original thinkers, such as Daniel Pink who forecasts the emergence of right over left brain thinkers. There is no denying a link between performance and happiness. But even as we agree there is a connection between happy workers and the bottom line, we can also predict that the profit motif will not diminish. Therefore, the task is to demonstrate that by helping employees thrive everyone benefits. There still remains the nagging question: How do we make employees happy?

Valuing happiness is gaining importance in other countries. In 1972 the King of Bhutan announced that gross national happiness is more important than gross national product, and that happiness is more important than prosperity. With forty-one countries engaged in measuring happiness, the topic is likely to have an impact.

According to *HBR* authors for the Happiness edition, the answer for U.S. companies is to involve employees in decision making, sharing information, and *minimizing incivility*. The first two are evident and discussed in other examples in this book. Incivility is not new and rarely talked about but gaining in strategic importance. Incivility in this context applies to leaders exercising power by berating employees publicly and similar humiliating acts. The most egregious is utilizing the fear factor of threatening dismissal.

Flatter organizations will go a considerable distance from

merely overcoming incivility in order to engage, encourage, and energize employees. Instead of being construed as a negative, speaking up is actually appropriate if employees are to act responsibly by challenging everything.

Chapter Nine: International Alliances

Anne Reilly advanced quickly at Loyola University in Chicago, Illinois. Starting as an Assistant Professor, in record speed she progressed to Full Professor and a Dean in the School of Business. After a two-year stint as Assistant Provost & Director of Faculty Administration, she has returned as Associate Dean to what is now the Quinlan Graduate School of Business at Loyola. Her teaching and research has involved organization change, work/family issues, and value-based leadership in a changing world.

Always at the top of students' faculty evaluations, she was invited to teach at the Loyola campus in Rome, as well as programs in China and Greece.

Loyola's strategic university plan includes increased interest in becoming more global. The university has had a campus in Rome since 1962. By increasing opportunities to study abroad, other programs have been made available. In keeping with a faith-based focus, attention has been drawn to underserved places such as Africa.

The university seeks to be relevant in the manner courses are offered: typical classroom, online, and hybrid. A link to recognizing the importance of learning styles, such as experiential learning and team interaction, is being considered with emphasis on how learning is internalized and utilized.

The university's intent to fulfill the need for knowledgeable, creative, and culturally sensitive graduates is becoming a priority. Universities, like other organizations, are faced with the need to break down historic roles in order to be viable in the future. Leading the way to breaking down barriers and establishing programs that enhance globalization naturally falls to Quinlan.

When teaching Change and Organization Development, Anne directs attention to how businesses must keep up the fast pace required in a competitive marketplace. Now that she has returned to the reorganized business school, she assists with international curriculum development, including the groundbreaking Intercontinental MBA program. Full-time students attend classes on three continents: Africa, South America, and Asia. Quinlan is focused on students who have the interest and require skills for international management and marketing positions.

Classes in Chicago are followed by opportunities to apply and live what is learned. The university connects their students with local businesses and faculty aligns with firms where internships can be arranged.

For winter break, partnering universities work with Quinlan to arrange programs in other countries. A connection with University of Arizona has led to opportunities in Thailand, Cambodia, and Vietnam. An eight-day spring break is being offered in Chile.

Linkages often occur because of Loyola's mission as a Jesuit school. For instance, in Vietnam where training is needed for nurses and hospital management, the university responded quickly.

Loyola is exploring other partners and locations that fit not only the need to develop skills for international organizations, but to serve what they call "marginalized" populations. The mission of the business school complements Loyola's intent to serve the underserved. This fit has been characteristic of Loyola for some time. It was one of the first universities to teach ethics as a required course in the business curriculum. A link with the nursing school is another example of objectives beyond the profit motif. Driven by a faith-based value system, what matters is "passion and involvement" and a desire to engage other people. The goal is to challenge both faculty and students to think differently.

Sustainability, as it relates to changing the organization for the future, is perceived as appropriate for the common good. People are invited to think beyond the present, to a business world of the future that coordinates faculty research and teaching. If looked at from this perspective, fundamental business practices are questioned and new practices are encouraged. That is the way change is embraced.

Anne has already noticed how engaged students are in this new context. She recalls two groups in one of her classes who prepared papers that reflect the drive to undertake research, analysis, and draw high-level actionable conclusions. Students are pragmatic and look for immediate applications of knowledge acquired.

Loyola's international faculty, drawn from many countries, including India, Korea and Croatia to name a few, is an asset. As a Catholic institution, it embraces diversity and reaches out to other religious groups. In fact, the oldest Hillel chapter at a Jesuit school is at Loyola Chicago. The faculty is aligned with professors in other universities that are critical in advancing global awareness. Even though they leave the day-to-day details connected with administration to others, they seek to be consulted and engaged in whatever is new. Anne, as a professor and a Dean, knows how to get the faculty on board for change; make them part of the process.

Cultural Literacy

Universities are beginning to offer global study programs, not just as add-ons, but as a means to prepare students for the complexities of doing business in foreign nations. The undergraduate junior year abroad programs available for generations have morphed into one-, two-, and even four-year separate sojourns worldwide. MBA students have been going abroad as part of their curriculum for some time. Instead of just one opportunity, many programs offer two or more international experiences. Indiana University in Bloomington has established a Center for the Study of Global Change to engage and develop faculty and staff to integrate innovation, interconnection, and internationalization into their teaching; the stated goal is to prepare students for employment.

There are also high schools where there is an emphasis on global consciousness. The School for International Studies in Brooklyn, New York, is an example of the mission to prepare students grades 6-12 to be "citizens of the world."

New York University has a wide variety of choices for graduate and undergraduate students seeking to be involved in global studies. Options include going to some or all of NYU's worldwide sites in Accra, Buenos Aires, Florence, London, Prague, and Shanghai. Faculty is encouraged to participate, conduct research, and engage in scholarly collaborations abroad.

Morgan, a student who has already completed studies in Europe and South America, shares her experiences in a blog entitled "One in (24) Million" from Shanghai. She writes about an excursion to Beijing, including observations about food, transportation, and street music. Back in Shanghai, she writes about adjacent towns and museums. Layered on liberal arts courses is the immersion into the daily life, the arts, music, economies, political environments, intercultural communication issues of each place visited, and the learning of at least one language.

Cultural literacy is essential if employees are to apply personal observation, research, and analysis to the complexities of doing business globally. Maya Hu-Chan and Brian O. Underhill in *Partnering, the New Face of Leadership* describe what is needed to partner with people in other cultures. They emphasize the importance of developing the next generation for this task. Openness to change, common values and motivations, embracement of new technology, virtual relationships resulting from colleagues in distant places, plus empowerment which comes from trust are the key factors they suggest for cross-cultural success.

The way for organizations to ensure that their employees in the near future have those critical assets is to align with universities and to enhance the experiences of students with internships. Alliances and collaborative projects with universities across the globe ensure that the courses will benefit all parties involved. Corporate survival is increasing dependent on employees who are culture sensitive.

The importance of language and culture in establishing meaningful transactions has been dramatized in movie and stage productions. *Lost in Translation* depicted on film the perils connected with long distance travel and language transactions. The Broadway show *Chinglish* highlights the plight of miscommunication in attempting to find common ground for negotiation.

Chapter Ten: Crossing the Pond Both Ways

The "jump across the pond" offers many lessons and many stories. The transition from working for a U.S. company to a foreign company is easier if English is the common language. Being comfortable in the multilingual setting of the headquarter country depends upon knowledge of, and respect for, cultural differences. Until recently, it was possible for a senior officer who served as the liaison in the U.S. to the headquarters abroad to feel like an entrepreneur operating independently, while keeping the home office appraised. However, changes in global corporations have reduced American autonomy at home. This is particularly evident in family businesses abroad, restructuring after decades to be competitive in the new marketplace.

Americans ready to challenge themselves by working for an international company will discover many differences in respect to how business is done. One example is a controlling level of confidentiality. Revealing company information is prohibited.

Human Resource issues regarding salary, training, development, and promotion present hurdles. In some ways, the U.S. is more capable than other countries in adapting to new structures, primarily in respect to strategic initiatives, social media, and teamwork. New technologies are forcing the creation of positions that did not exist before. Identifying talent and developing people is gaining priority status.

Foreign companies that have traditional hierarchical structures are realizing that they must consider alternatives.

Worldwide organizations are revising their structures. Collaboration is gaining momentum. Task forces are being assembled to coordinate decision-making across national and international facilities.

International organizations are realizing that their deeply entrenched planning methodologies and policies are outdated. Developing a strategic plan for working in, or with the U.S., involves assessing the percentage of the market that the foreign company can reasonably achieve. Research is recognized as critical in order to identify opportunities and mobilize a diverse workforce.

How do foreign nationals fare when they come to America? They may know the language but not the legal or subtle interpretations of policies and procedures. This is especially significant in financial organizations. While high-end customers seek to do business with the top officer of a company, sometimes they must wait until that person reaches a higher level of confidence and competence. Access to the most senior person is often impeded due to home office stipulations regarding the level of decision-making afforded their foreign offices. Delays in home office approvals get in the way of time-pressed customers.

American employees also experience frustration when home country leadership is repeatedly replaced. The revolving door of chief executives diminishes collaboration internally, as the work staff must constantly divert time and energy to understand the style and management objectives of each new chief.

U.S. employees can be equally dismayed by the lag time for getting approvals which ultimately affects morale. Some foreign countries may be indifferent to issues related to morale. For instance, while there are a few countries where there is a willing trade-off between time on the job versus money, other incentives are ignored. Training, development, and performance feedback are rarely considered high priority. Therefore, in order to be considered worthy of promotion, the tendency is to concentrate on short-term results. The negative consequence to this practice is that setting and achieving long-term objectives for the company is neglected.

What has been perceived as insensitivity to the people-related side of the business is exemplified in a poignant situation recalled by an American working for an international corporation. The chief officer brought employees and their families together for a Christmas dinner. Before the event, everyone was instructed to attend a meeting. The chief executive's speech was short; he said that the law requires events of this nature to be business-oriented, which is why they were assembled—to meet that requirement. And then he dismissed the group. It was an important opportunity missed. The organization had finished a very successful year, and instead of using this time and this gathering to thank everyone, including the families for their support, he seemed to scorn the organization's debt to its hardworking, achievement-oriented employees and their affected families. Had he praised his employees and expressed his appreciation, he would have increased motivation and promoted further engagement in the company's success for the forthcoming year.

Issues from the Other Side

From a very different perspective, Angela D'Aversa, a retired senior executive with Borg Warner, a U.S. company with facilities in sixty countries, reflects on her experiences. Hired originally as a Human Resource manager for the corporate office, she ultimately was promoted to Vice President of Human Resources with global HR responsibility. She had two roles. As a member of the executive team, she was responsible for helping the facilities with issues related to human resources. As part of the strategy board, she worked with the country manager, plant personnel, and other local employees to assess capability and progress in achieving business goals.

Work in so many different cultures required preparation, confidence, courage, and discipline. She said that gaining attention and respect begins by having a strong belief in what she was doing, the will to stick her neck out, and to speak up.

Preparation was her first mandate. Before going to a new site, she and her team used tools such as GlobeSmart® to learn history and culture, including such aspects as card presentation, gift giving, and even what to drink at business meetings. It was important getting people working with her, both at home and across the pond, to be involved and invested. This led to fewer mistakes, correct conclusions, and better assumptions.

Her purpose was to build management skills, and she developed curriculums to that end to assist locals. A number of the countries did not have Human Resource departments, making her job more complex and necessitating the introduction of training programs and tools needed to comply with company standards.

Over time she developed several axioms that highlighted what is different when working outside the U.S. Number one is that there are many words that are interpreted differently. Even though English is the business language across the company, the same words have different interpretations. One such word is "profit," and confusion around it can lead to trouble. To overcome this confusion she started by asking questions to clarify meaning and understanding.

Safety is an area of keen importance for a U.S. company for both humane and business reasons. However, because it is of lesser value in many other countries, local managers fight the cost. In order to respond to the corporate mandate, Human Resources steps in to help local managers overseas solve the problem and institute a workable solution.

Sometimes the difference in cultures shows up in unusual ways. Angela recalls a dinner in Germany when the Americans had ordered dinner prior to a program the next day. The food was slow in being served. Those from the U.S. who had flown in were expecting dinner to proceed in a timely fashion. When queried regarding the delay, the local management team indicated that what was regarded as slow was in keeping with the German way, which prizes conversation over dinner rather than speed. He said Americans tend to gobble their food, in contrast to the three to four hour dinners that are the norm in Germany. Their German hosts felt it was somewhat insulting that Americans do not allocate enough time for relationship-building over a meal.

Change is coming, but it takes time, Angela maintains. There have been attempts at restructuring, mostly in terms of rethinking where the locus of control should be. Typically in a down market, companies tend to centralize in order to control loss of revenue, and centralizing tends to reinforce hierarchies.

The other side of the pond resembles what is happening in the U.S. and worldwide, demonstrating the essential need to mobilize in order to deal with escalating complexity. Cultural sensitivity both ways is a leap forward.

Chapter Eleven: There is Always More to Learn

As a business consultant and psychologist, Carole Parker has had the rare opportunity to work with a vast array of clients while they are experiencing a multitude of issues. Because she has been doing this since 1981, she is a reliable source for identifying problems and pressures in corporate America.

Conversations with Carole are never boring; she has experienced much and reads extensively. As a PhD Clinical Psychologist, she has worked with companies, numerous private individuals, and small groups across the country. Her perspective with respect to change, creativity, and globalization has been formed as a result of how individuals face and cope with these forces in their environment. For instance, she sees a significant difference between how people in their twenties and thirties react to travel and residence abroad than those in their forties and fifties. The enticement of life in another country can be a great draw for those newly graduated individuals who seek novel experiences and the opportunity to learn new languages and cultures. However, she points out once there is the prospect of family, the need for work/life balance dominates decision-making.

Globalization, she asserts, can be brutal and play havoc with people's lives. For companies who do business from their offices in the U.S., there are the same demands on learning language and culture with the added dimension of availability across a 24-hour time span. The pressures are great, but not as overwhelming as moving to a distant country where shots are required, amenities are few, and healthcare is questionable.

Initial illusions become tarnished quickly.

From her point of view, leadership across organizations is focused on getting things done, delivering the goods, and achieving results. Managers are expected to adapt to circumstances (which often translates to a reduced workforce or limited resources). There is an expectation that managers have business acumen and are financially and politically savvy. Their primary goal is to achieve fiscal objectives, but how that is to be accomplished is less clear.

The current marketplace does not encourage people to make waves, and therefore any inclination to take risks is diminished. This is at odds with a basic desire of executives to have interesting and engaging work that motivates them to act and operate as entrepreneurs.

In her practice she sees many people who are looking for higher levels of well-being and healthier ways of functioning as leaders and individuals. Organizations seek talent and the ability to simplify the complex; individuals seek creative excitement, opportunities to work with the best in their field, and challenges. How are these divergent positions to be reconciled? Carole maintains that everyone must lead in business and in life. Her credo is "clarity, courage, and humanity."

Further Insights

The psychological point of view provides insights into how people are dealing with the powerful forces of change coming from so many different places at the same time. How does anyone maintain equilibrium in the face of so much turmoil? The book, *The Psychology of Leadership: New Perspectives and Research*, edited by David M. Messick and Roderick M. Kramer, presents the thoughts of esteemed academics and researchers on the subject of leadership. One author, Michael A. Hogg, who looks at social identity and leadership, affirms that when the relationship between leaders and followers is consensual, stable and legitimate, with mutual goals, people feel a strong sense of belonging.

In *Breakpoint and Beyond: Mastering the Future Today*, George Land and Beth Jarman approach the topic differently from their backgrounds in anthropology and education. They see "unparalleled opportunity" in a time that requires change and inspires an altered worldview. Transformation is positive, not just for a few but for those who are able to rediscover their creative spirit. They see a time of renewed vitality and original solutions. By overcoming what the authors describe as traps, such as "measurement becoming the mission, spreadsheet mentality, tight control, [and] information filtering" the reinvented organization will soar.

At the Frontier: What's Next?

The stories in the book reveal the best of leadership today. Those interviewed provide the pathway to the future because they have identified the constraints in the current environment and responded effectively. As they seek to position their organizations for an unpredictable world, they will reap advantages from what they have learned, but they will encounter other serious and unanticipated hurdles. What follows is a design for assisting organizations through transition to the future by maximizing the only sustainable competitive advantage—people.

The first most significant and necessary step is to *engage* people in the pursuit of their organization's strategic goals. Command and control structures perpetuate the obsession to achieve immediate number-related objectives, while at the same time sabotaging innovation. The constant quest for position and power in a hierarchical structure leaves the most important and knowledgeable people out of the dialogue. Furthermore, it alienates instead of engaging those who seek to collaborate and contribute.

Structure influences how organizations create cultures and related workspace designs that either foster or inhibit collaboration and the exchange of ideas. Tackling structure and culture is the *first consideration* for an organization that seeks to step up to the demands of global competition, mindboggling change, and the perpetual need for innovation. While turning the pyramid upside down may appear dramatic, drastic, and difficult, the evidence is strong that creativity increases as an organization gets flatter. The need to take risks and find optimal, and sometimes unconventional, solutions is enhanced. Since the watchword for the future is newness, altering the context and environment is the priority.

Collaboration breeds engagement and commitment. Getting rid of silos and other barriers enables partnering that capitalizes on knowledge and experience. Establishing a culture that promotes new learning, exploration, and discovery encourages continual refreshment of skill-sets and broadening of perspectives. Cross-functional interaction and cooperation is enhanced as is collective and mutual accountability.

Relationship building, seeking synergies across organizations, and developing alliances and reciprocal agreements within and outside the organization are critical in this drive for success. One such arrangement might well be with universities providing online courses and other programs for learning languages, cultures, and history to bolster global affiliations.

Attention to work-life balance and acceptance of the organization's role in respect to wellness heightens commitment and supports the coveted engagement.

This is not a three-, four- or five-step program; it is part of a simultaneous equation that starts with the most basic objectives and the belief that one aspect leads quickly to others since they are interconnected.

Globalization influences leadership in the U.S. in a number of significant ways: buying or selling goods or services, establishing and sustaining mergers and acquisitions, foreign vs. domestic investing, and hiring or developing skilled people, and determining the locus and extent of authority. Knowing more languages and learning how cultures differ so that meaningful relationships can be made happens only with effort, research, and sensitivity. The choices are to hire people internally and develop them, hire from outside those who are experts, or hire in strategic international locations.

The most basic issue in this global, high-tech environment is how to handle complexities related to strategic planning, decision making, identifying and securing talent, building alliances, branding, pricing, marketing, and rewarding personnel. Obviously a single leader cannot undertake all this. Partnering and collaboration are replacing command and control hierarchies across the globe. Cultures that promote thinking and empowerment provide incentive for "doers" to contribute on a higher level. Those who create alliances that promote genuine mutual regard will have the advantage over companies that ignore this imperative.

The leaders who are profiled have learned to be agile and to go against the tide when that is indicated. They experienced breakthroughs in their efforts to ignite and maintain momentum. Their insights are valuable, but what they learned should not serve as a formula but as a stimulus for current and aspiring leaders to frame a new leadership model that is in sync with this new era. Where does change need to occur? Culture and communication are starters.

Culture

Gary Hamel, a prominent business author says that "when you dismantle the pyramid, you drain much of the poison out of an organization."

An inverted pyramid calls for multiple changes in organizational culture and communication. The following outlines what must be considered to achieve a reinvented organization capable of having a major presence on the local and the world scene. What you get is greater initiative, deeper expertise, better decisions, and increased flexibility.

The elements of culture entails how people are perceived, views regarding how power is distributed, how engagement and alignment bring together formerly disparate parts of an organization, how workplace redesign will enable and enhance collaboration, how simplifying reports and documents frees up time for higher-level decision-making, how information sharing strengthens every part of an organization, why providing a safe environment for speaking up is a force for continuous organization improvement, and individual development.

Some of the core precepts are listed below:

People are number one: This is the basic principle that ensures a sustainable competitive advantage. Clever people are magnets for other clever people.

Attention to well-being: When people know that they are worthy of the organization's focus on them as humans with personal needs they are much more likely to commit themselves and engage.

Assess power in a new way: Not as position power, not authority over others, not by determining the mission/vision and setting objectives for others, but instead partnering, building relationships, finding synergies, inspiring innovation, creativity, and bold thinking.

Give authentic empowerment: Simply treating employees well isn't empowering them. The danger of highly centralized, hierarchical organizations treating their employees well is motivational, but not necessarily empowering to the employees individually. Executives' words imply "you're empowered" while their actions say "you're empowered as long as you get approval first."

Add synchronicity into the organization's vocabulary: It is the result of high levels of engagement and alignment across the organization and it will make a difference.

Streamline by breaking down silos: By reducing competition for resources and eliminating contentious conflicts of interest, time and money is saved and motivation is increased. Flatter structures shift attention to achieving what is beneficial for the whole organization.

Simplify and shorten reports: Encourage well-thought-out and succinct documents. Eliminate the creation of long presentations.

Share information: Open the books to all employees so they know the role they can play in achieving strategic goals.

Provide a safe environment: People need to be able to challenge, speak up, disagree, suggest, and alert others to problems and prospective pitfalls.

Learn to and help others to thrive on ambiguity: The point is not just tolerating ambiguity it is dealing with ambiguity collectively, so that better alternatives surface to identify optimal solutions. Similarly, when more than one person assesses risk, the decision-making process is improved. Individuals who thrive are not rushed to quick decisions.

Foster knowledge of related technologies: Support personal growth and willingness to contribute to the growth and development of others. Encourage and support credit and certificate courses in universities. Share articles, books, videos, and other pertinent material to keep everyone updated. Create an organization that values openness, experimentation, continuous learning, and investigation.

Promote discovery: Provide opportunities for stimulating thought. Frame and ask open-ended questions. Question the prevailing wisdom to elicit new possibilities.

Resist bold plans for achieving ever-higher revenue goals: This can be an excuse for abandoning innovation that could lead to competitor advantage.

Move from a past-oriented mindset that refers to best practices: At a time when agility is a primary asset, looking forward is the only correct direction. Meeting the future will soon make what was done yesterday ancient history.

Help others to think of themselves as entrepreneurs, as owners with a high stake in outcomes: Expect, prepare, and look out for leaders to emerge. Make involvement, inclusion, and innovation your collective motto.

Circulate articles regarding industry and global trends: Keeping your teams up-to-date on the latest information enables employees to reflect on ways to position the organization in an ever-changing environment.

Communication

According to Terry Lundgren, Chairman, President, and CEO of Macy's, "The only way to address uncertainty is to communicate and communicate. And when you think you've just about got to everybody, then communicate some more."

Establishing an ongoing dialogue is essential in the fast-changing interconnected world. The following outlines ways to communicate that utilize tools, some of which are new and some older that might have been overlooked.

Networking has been a boon to those who have experienced the benefits. Several of those profiled in this book reveal the advantages gained by reaching out to others in different sectors to enhance their range of choices that may be complementary or unconventional to arrive at better solutions. It is essential to reach out to counterparts in university settings, association meetings, and personal networks of trusted friends.

PowerPoint, initially developed by a former Berkeley PhD student who envisioned a user-friendly visual method of presentation, captivated the business world. The precision, use of technology, and capability for data distribution that PowerPoint offers began as an asset. Fortune 100 companies, the military, and even grade school classes have been using the program as a primary means of communicating. Unfortunately the method promotes linear thinking, which suggests that problems are resolved sequentially. This and other limitations cause disillusionment to be inevitable, and today many audiences express their boredom and displeasure during a PowerPoint presentation by texting, checking e-mail, and tweeting. The hours of preparation and the time spent watching is time spent poorly. It ends up being more style than substance and the disturbing typical outcome is at the completion of the presentation when the audience leaves the room. The meaning of the data is left for each individual to disseminate separately. There is no analysis or discussion. An opportunity is missed.

On April 27, 2010, the front page of the New York Times showed a PowerPoint diagram that was to be used by generals in a forthcoming meeting. The topic was Afghan stability. The intention was to portray the complexity of the situation; however, the diagram was so overwhelming in its density, it led to the next article, entitled "We Have Met the Enemy and He is PowerPoint." The tool itself is not the culprit and is useful to impart facts and figures; however, it would be better served as a stimulus for exploration and sharing ideas and as a springboard for dialogue.

Innovation

With newness as the watchword of this fast-paced, highly competitive, worldwide marketplace, it is surprising to witness the confusion experienced by many organizations in respect to the simple question, "What constitutes innovation in my business?" Being innovative has been bred out of so many organizations; what little there is, is usually an extension of what is already being done to make the process cheaper or faster. Long-term employees who have suggested new products or new markets have frequently seen their attempt at newness either ignored, discounted, or simply forgotten. After a few suggestions, it's back to business as usual. Another confounding factor is that due to the need to streamline (translation: reduce headcount), employees are working longer hours and frequently performing the work of two people. This leaves little opportunity for or interest in creativity.

Neither leaders nor the workforce are expected to think like entrepreneurs. A few organizations, realizing that competition requires the introduction of previously untried actions, address the employees' fear of failure by saying, "We want you to experiment," and "It is OK to fail," and "We expect mistakes will be made." Unfortunately, what employees quickly learn is that one mistake is acceptable, two are questionable, and three is out the door. Risk is not really tolerated. What has started to pass for innovation is resourcefulness—that is applying minor tweaks to attain a minimal competitive advantage.

What would be different if American enterprise started to make the changes necessary to compete in this new arena?

Starting with people, the only lasting competitive advantage would entail hiring or identifying "clever people." Leadership for this population is incompatible with organization hierarchies. Players know what they are worth and are in demand; therefore, they are scornful of hierarchies and impatient with layers of management. They want an environment that provides a high degree of autonomy with room to explore and even to fail. Because they are connected to outside networks, they have greater knowledge regarding what the competition is doing and thus greater personal mobility. This new breed of worker whose knowledge and experience has been nurtured in environments where debate is a norm is intolerant of cultures where challenges are considered "insubordination."

Start-Ups

Start-ups, the most formidable leap into the future, involve an amount of bravery rare in current U.S. businesses, which can be explained by the continuous pressure on leaders to achieve financial goals connected to short-term timelines. To even introduce a new product demands a level of confidence that can be quickly eroded in the face of clamor for *revenue now* rather than *profit later*. I have seen organizations tiptoe into new ventures holding the internal entrepreneurs accountable but providing very little support. A company used to reversing downturns quickly with an advertisement, predictably produces quick results and is not likely to be patient for weeks, months, or a year to see results. Beleaguered internal innovators are cautioned to "manage perceptions" so that the impatient leaders will not close down the new venture. Newness in corporate America is mainly conversation with little action.

In other places, Israel, for a small nation, has numerous start-ups with results that are financially successful within relatively short time periods. What is different at these companies is instructive: a workforce that challenges leadership, is collaborative in planning and execution, and has access to advanced technology and pertinent data. What would be "rank and file" in the U.S. has become the moving force in Israel, allowing start-ups to benefit from soldier training that includes thinking globally, gaining and utilizing requisite skills quickly, and undertaking challenges that result in superior outcomes.

According to *Start-Up Nation: The Story of Israel's Economic Miracle* written by Dan Senor and Saul Singer, Israel has earned worldwide distinction for creating a workforce that is prepared to question, risk, challenge, and learn how to use cutting-edge technology for an expanding economy. The two or three years most Israelis spend in the army enable them to confront and capitalize on ambiguity and to excel at experimentation. They think in terms of team and collaboration but can also be independent and entrepreneurial.

Support also comes from research centers, proximity to universities, and a large, continually growing talent pool. The movement away from hierarchies has produced the kind of confidence and bravery that makes newness happen.

Organizational Structure

Organization structure makes a difference. USG Corporation found that a matrix structure promoted the kind of collaboration needed to address a crisis situation. The hospital in Santa Cruz, California, created cross-functional units, rather than the usual functionally based hospital structure. This enabled the unit heads to work cooperatively under great pressure and stress.

For generations the organization chart neatly represented reporting relationships. The hierarchy was clearly in evidence and everyone knew their place. After a while, changes came so rapidly that updating charts was taking too much time. When staffing changes were needed, leaders would think more about the position being considered, rather than the people who might fill it.

Computers make updating easy, and most organizations still cling to chart mentality. Nevertheless, alternatives are being proposed that will base organizational positions from the perspective of maximizing attainment of strategic goals.

Frances Hesselbein was CEO of the Girl Scouts national organization from 1976 to 1990. She made leadership history, not only because of the positive results she achieved, but because she was innovative in structuring her organization. Instead of a traditional chart, she established a new structure with people and functions across three concentric circles with the CEO in the center. She maintains that a "circular management liberates energy and the human spirit." The first response to her views regarding "letting go of hierarchy" was to complain that it only works with nonprofit organizations. In time for-profit organizations found her precepts to be useful. Peter Drucker, a leadership icon, said that "Frances Hesselbein could manage any company in America." She banned the hierarchy and "took people out of boxes and moved them into a flat, more flexible and fluid system." She favored a dispersed and diverse leadership that shared responsibility by building partnerships.

Workplace Design

Workplace design is critical. Eliminating cubicles that are alienating and distancing is step one. Multiple conference rooms of different sizes to accommodate small groups and work stations for team projects are superior replacements.

Architects are responding to the emerging interest in workplace design that will support interaction. Office furniture manufacturers are following suit. Some have proposed plans and alternatives that allow different work modes, such as collaboration, teamwork, client interaction, and socialization. Those companies paying attention to the impact of design have reduced the number of offices and increased open areas and places for impromptu meetings. Google, DreamWorks, and GE are among those companies redesigning office areas to accommodate different work styles and maximize the talents of their employees. While booths and conference areas are provided for private conversations, roaming is encouraged. This allows for discovery of what others are engaged in and taking note of what is relevant. This kind of openness advances mutual objectives.

Spending an afternoon with an architect, whose specialty is interior design, heightened the realization that organizations must be alert to workplace design in respect to function and feel. Lisa Kincaid is a Principal with Gastinger Walker Harden Kincaid + Malone. Her interest in architecture was sparked years ago when she was hired as a secretary. Her intuitive skills became rapidly evident when she was able to resolve a client's crisis. This increased her value to the firm to the extent that her university degrees were subsidized by them. She earned the first of many awards for her interest and aptitude in creating workplace designs for corporate interiors, using creative lighting, colors, and fabrics. Her approach involves careful planning and discussion with the client in order to meet their goals.

Lisa instinctively knew that compatibility between client, design, and achievement of goals is essential. However, it took several years for the corporate world to catch up and embrace change. The trappings that came with hierarchies such as corner offices, offices with windows, and executive conference rooms are hard to give up. Symbolic gestures relating to status is prevalent in many organizations and is associated with power and the perception of importance.

Cubicles with fluorescent lighting maybe more economical but do little to advance organization strategic goals. As younger people come onboard, more sophisticated technology is available, and the demand for interaction increases. It is obvious that something has to be done to facilitate, rather than impede, collaboration and entrepreneurial thinking. The landscape is beginning to change, reducing the emphasis on title and office location. However, contrary to an acknowledged pursuit of creativity and innovation, many employees are still operating in stifling environments.

The link between performance and office space ignited momentum. At first, manufacturers offered variations on the old theme by using more glassed-in spaces and improved lighting. As they conducted serious research, they learned the critical connection between productivity and work environment.

For Lisa, now is the time to finally match interior design with corporation work processes and strategic goals. She creates workstations that match the nature of the work. When two or three people are working on a project, their space can include one or two computer monitors for each person. Chairs are moveable. Tables can be adjusted to higher or shorter positions as needed. Desk lamps replace overhead lighting. Since offices are increasingly paperless, storage is of little importance. There is what Lisa calls "we space and I space." In fact, one manufacturer refers to areas where several stations are connected as "collaboration areas." There are numerous conference rooms, some large, some small, usually glassed in. Some areas have tall, narrow, bar-like tables, a few with barstools, so that brief sit-down or stand-up meetings can occur.

Studies show that windows affect mental alertness and productivity. Since daylight is important, workstation separations are designed to let light in from nearby windows. Glass and other see-through fabrics are utilized, as are fabrics that reduce sound (thereby increasing privacy) but still admit light.

Glass walls, in fact most walls, are demountable so that change can quickly be achieved. As a result almost everything is variable.

White boards are prevalent, as are graphics on walls—some for artistic purposes; other walls can be written on for information purposes or to share ideas related to work or employee interests.

These developing workstation environments represent a new mindset regarding how to meet individual, group, and organization goals. Since employees are working longer hours, comfort is important. Most essential from a business standpoint is that they are able to maximize their research, analysis, reviewing, listening, and presenting opportunities. Conversion in space design does not immediately eliminate the hierarchy, but it does tend to flatten the organization so that ideas and dialogue are more readily exchanged.

Tools

Scenarios

In 1991 a book by Peter Schwartz, *The Art of the Long View: Planning for the Future in an Uncertain World*, introduced organizations to scenario building, a tool used to conduct strategic planning. Essentially it provides a format for members from across the organization to meet with the primary task of developing what-ifs regarding the future. Several groups meet independently to develop stories or scenarios that seem plausible based on their personal insights plus addition research. The concept is used continuously by Royal Dutch Shell and many other companies. Looking into the future in this manner has produced sharper and more reliable results. Separate groups consider what Schwartz calls the "driving forces: society, technology, economics, politics and environment." In recent years companies have added new forces and have expanded the research methodology. The concept adds extra value in dealing with the magnitude of change derived from technology and a globally competitive and interconnected world.

Skill Banks

Keeping data in each employee's personnel file that included skills beyond what was required for their current positions, including fluency in other languages and other core competencies was a practice introduced a few decades ago. This endeavor ebbed due to the burden of keeping the files updated. However, the computer age has made this ongoing, continually updatable database achievable and reliable.

The new version of skill banks allows the organization to easily access and tap into employee knowledge, such as second (and third) languages (with level of fluency), technology competencies used in previous positions or gained independently, and project leadership for either profit or nonprofit organizations. Employees may have high-level knowledge and skills learned as a result of personal interests or gained through religious or community volunteer work.

What is critical now is that there is an immediately obtainable data bank with the capacity to access skills that can benefit both the organization and the individual. For example, if an organization needs someone who speaks a particular foreign language, from Spanish, French, Russian, German, Vietnamese, Chinese, Hmong, or even Sign Language, that person might be right at hand.

Well beyond language, a skill bank can track the presence of those who have technological skills or who are training formally in a classroom, learning online, or independently. Awards or commendations earned, association membership and/or leadership, courses taken, credits, and certificates earned can all be part of the employee's file.

Two goals are accomplished: what individuals learn outside the organization may one day be timely and productively put to use and the organization endorses a learning mindset and supports and encourages employees to continue their development.

NGT

The Nominal Group Technique (NGT) was developed in the 1970s by two U.S. professors, André Delbecq and Andrew Van de Ven, who sought a better way to brainstorm in a group setting. They created a process that many organizations, both for-profit and nonprofit, have used to learn the concerns and interests of groups without the negatives that inevitably occur with other methods. Brainstorming in business settings rarely leads to the desired results because the dynamic of most groups defeats the purpose. For instance, a group is called together, usually without much advance notice, to discuss a sensitive topic and to specifically consider issues or possible actions to be taken. The basic premise is that groups are able to provide avenues for further discussion or action. The topic is presented and the leader asks for ideas. Some people speak up while others remain silent.

Unfortunately there is often someone who has too much to say and is intimidating, either in manner or title particularly if the group has different levels of management represented. The imbalance of the participants can deter the success of brainstorming.

The NGT is a group process with a definite purpose stated upfront. It starts with what is referred to as "silent generation" when each person is asked to write a list of their ideas for dealing with the topic, thus giving them time to collect their thoughts. Then the leader goes around the room taking the first point from each person's list and writing what was offered on a tear sheet.

There is no discussion except to ask for clarity. Each point is assigned a number. By round three or four, ideas are duplicated, and some choose to piggyback on an earlier item. The tear sheets multiply and are hung around the conference room.

Participants review the tear sheets independently. There is either a private voting that is handed in to the leader, or people walk around and vote on the tear sheets. The end result is that the five or six top-ranked points made by the group motivate action. It is called nominal due to the fact there is no discussion.

The conclusion is positive in that there has been no open

conflict, people are not intimidated in putting their ideas forward, and in addition to the top ranked ideas, there are pages of worthwhile ideas for future work. The creators of NGT, unlike many designers, did not copyright it.

Improvisation

Jazz is not often considered a tool for business organizations but is starting to show promise as a way to help organizations embrace innovation. Mary Jo Hatch, a professor of organization theory in the UK, discussed this approach in a 1999 article, entitled "Exploring the Empty Spaces of Organizing: How Improvisational Jazz Helps Redescribe Organizational Structure." In it she describes using improvisation as a metaphor to demonstrate how creativity emerges when people are totally engaged in something of enduring value. Improvisation embodies structure, ambiguity, and emotion. In jazz the tune is built from what the leader starts, and new musical ideas are encouraged and included. Space is provided for contributions by others; listening and responding is essential to keep the ideas going and cohesive. Roles are swapped and because of the intense listening there is an increased amount of predictability. When the musicians find their groove they internalize and lock in so they can perform the same tune again. They lead and follow. They know when to solo and when to support. They switch between leading and backing. It is fairly intense and engaged teamwork. The process provokes imagination and creativity.

Jazz offers a way to understand how de-layering can occur in an organization. Sustainable alliances and networks can evolve out of shared action. When there is communication and collaboration, like the best jazz, the result is powerful.

Acknowledgements

My daughter, Marla Jacobson, has been a vital partner in this year-long book writing effort. Originally one of those who urged me to write a book, she became its proofreader, editor, researcher, and computer expert. I can never thank her enough. There are others whose support is appreciated. Bob Levin, who read my book concept and immediately put me in touch with Ron Goldfarb, his friend who subsequently became my agent. Ron helped me to clarify and continuously sharpen my message and then persevered in finding the right publishing fit. Also Les Jacobson, for his professional editing, drawn from newspaper and book writing experience. Sheldon Witcoff, for his constant encouragement and belief in me, and Sara Chwatt, who over many glasses of Malbec in Buenos Aires, convinced me I could and should write a book. I want to thank family and friends who have championed my ideas, especially Sandra, Chuck, and Lisa Kincaid, Sharon Morton, Marilyn Levin, Patsy Winicour, Linda Bliwas, and Fran Lippitz.

Over the last 20-plus years, I have been fortunate to consult with senior leadership in many organizations for periods of time ranging from three to twenty years. During the last ten years, I served primarily as an Executive Coach. Thanks especially to my clients and colleagues, many of whom have become friends. When asked if they would agree to be interviewed for the book, each immediately said "yes," not "maybe" or "I'll have to think about it." In that spirit of openness, this book was able to reveal how they have contributed to their various organizations and what we can learn from them.

About the Author

Marilyn Jacobson graduated from the University of Michigan with a major in English Literature. She then earned an MA from Northwestern University in English Literature and taught at Kendall Junior College, introducing courses in the Short Story and Best Seller Literature. After teaching at Roosevelt University she returned to Northwestern University for a PhD. Upon completion she submitted and directed a Federal Grant for the Adult Career Advocates Project and was an Assistant Professor at Northwestern. Two years later, she submitted and directed a grant from the Illinois Department of Commerce and Community Affairs. During this period, she served on the Illinois Governor's Education, Training, and Work Committee.

Subsequently, she had dual academic positions at the University of Illinois at Chicago in the School of Business and the School of Public Health. As an Assistant Professor, she taught MBA students in organization development, human resource management, and strategic planning. For the School of Public Health as an Adjunct Associate Professor, she conducted yearly seminars on Consulting in Healthcare Settings.

As an Adjunct Associate Professor at Loyola University for eleven years in the MBA and Executive MBA programs, she taught Organization Development and the capstone Strategic Planning course. At the same time, she consulted with numerous organizations in the U.S. and abroad covering a variety of industries including health care systems, individual hospitals, retail and manufacturing organizations in addition to law firms, and the governments of New York State and Indonesia.

Marilyn currently lives in Chicago and enjoys traveling extensively and continuing her consulting practice.

Made in the USA
Charleston, SC
28 May 2013